FOLK WOODCARVING

FOLK WOODCARVING

Compiled By Wang Kangsheng

 FOREIGN LANGUAGES PRESS

First Edition 2009

ISBN 978-7-119-04679-2

©Foreign Languages Press, Beijing, China, 2009

Published by

Foreign Languages Press

24 Baiwanzhuang Road, Beijing 100037, China

http: //www. flp. com. cn

Distributed by

China International Book Trading Corporation

35 Chegongzhuang Xilu, Beijing 100044, China

P.O. Box 399, Beijing, China

Printed in the People's Republic of China

Contents

Furnishings and Furniture / 97

Traditional Folk Implements / 121

Daily-use Articles / 127

Religious Woodcarvings / 131

INTRODUCTION

Woodcarving is a representative form of traditional art. Generally, woodcarvings are made of a kind of fine, firm, not easily warping wood, such as *nanmu*, red sandalwood, camphor wood, Chinese little leaf box, cedar wood, ginkgo, eagle-wood, mahogany or longan wood, as material, with motifs of different figures or forms for ornaments or practical works of art. Works of art carved with tree roots in natural forms are called "tree root sculptures."

Woodcraft is classified in accordance with usage of woodcarvings for structural, furnishing or religious purposes, or for appreciation and practical use, etc.; and, in accordance with carving techniques, such as line carving, shallow relief, alto-relivo, open-work carving, three-dimensional carving, etc. In their creation, a variety of carving methods are often used for one work.

Wooden horse:
Western Han Dynasty,
Wuwei, Gansu Province

Wooden monkey:
Western Han Dynasty,
Wuwei, Gansu

Color-painted
wooden figurine:
Mawangdui No.1
Han Dynasty tomb,
Changsha, Hunan
Province

Painted wooden horse:
Western Han,
Wuwei, Gansu

1. Historical Evolution of China's Woodcraft

Woodcarvings appeared in prehistoric civilization. An 11cm-long wood-carved fish unearthed in the Hemudu ruins site in Yuyao County, Zhejiang Province was made 6,000 to 7,000 years ago, the earliest woodcarving work discovered in China.

From the Shang and Zhou dynasties to the Spring and Autumn and the Warring States periods (16th century to 221 BC), which saw the transition from slave society to feudal society, many craftspeople gradually shook off the yoke of slavery, and became woodcarving artisans with relative freedom. This change provided the social foundation for the development of woodcarving arts. Lu Ban, a great carpenter, was an outstanding representative of the craftsmen of that time. To date, on Chinese New Year's Day or other festivals, woodcarving artists still kneel down by a tablet to venerate Lu Ban.

In the Warring States Period (475-221 BC), large numbers of wooden figurines were used to replace actual persons (in ancient China, live persons such as wife, concubines or attendants were buried alive with the dead emperors or high-ranking officials). These wooden figurines were of simple shape and in sketch form. On the utensils of that time were found many vividly shaped wood-carved animals. These wooden figurines and woodcarvings reflect that woodcraft in the Warring States Period was still in an early stage of development.

In terms of the period of the Qin and Han dynasties (221 BC-220 AD), numerous wooden figurines have been unearthed from Han tombs in grave mounds in Gansu Province's Wuwei, Mawangdui in Changsha, Hunan Province, and Hubei Province's Jiangling and Yunmeng. The carving methods were rough, yet in terms of both figure and spirit they appear quite lifelike. Of these, the wood-carved figurines in Wuwei are of a unique style, quite extraordinary due to the use of their highly concise carving technique. Their shapes are rough yet striking and succinct, capturing instant dynamic movement in a range of designs of human figures and animals, giving them both form and spirit, with motion residing in stillness. These works reflect that artistic woodcarvings during the period of the Qin and Han dynasties reached a very high level.

In the period of the Northern and Southern Dynasties (420-589), while the north was keenly carving out grottoes, the south was engaged in large-scale construction of temples and monasteries, and the prevalence of carvings of the Buddha and other religious woodcarvings promoted the development of woodcarving arts. Legend has it that sculptor Dai Kui of the Southern Dynasty once used an entire huge tree trunk to carve a 500cm-high statue of the Eternal Buddha. In the period of the Six Dynasties (222-589), Zhejiang Province became the center of celadon-ware production, in which celadon ornamental techniques included carving, embossing and block-printing. Among woodcarvers were specialists engaged in engraving various types of molds, while improvements in porcelain techniques also boosted the development of woodcarving arts.

During the Tang Dynasty (618-907), woodcarving arts began to develop in realist directions. Woodcarving subjects became increasingly wide-ranging, including human figures, deities such as the Buddha, flowers and birds, fowls and animals, covering every theme. Woodcarving techniques also promoted the development of block-printing techniques. The Tang Dynasty also invented the technique of carving with the knife edge after japanning, which is now called "picking out red," "picking out yellow" and "picking out black." It is said that Monk Xuanzang (602-664), of the Tang Dynasty, used the block-printing technique to print many images of Samantabhadra, allowing for popularization. The extant printed copies from the Tang Dynasty include the *Diamond Sutra*, reverentially created for his parents by Wang Jie in the ninth year of the reign of Emperor Yi Zong (860-874). A printed copy (about 30 sq cm) of the *Dharani Sutra*, unearthed in a Tang-dynasty tomb in Chengdu, Sichuan Province, was carved with a statue of Buddha and Sanskrit sutras.

The woodcarving techniques of the Song Dynasty (960-1279) became increasingly mature, their shape, realistic writing and aesthetics becoming quite superb and widely used in buildings and ornamentation. For example, the statue of Maitreya Buddha, in Wanfuge Hall of the Yonghe Lamasery in Beijing, was carved using red sandalwood three meters in diameter, with the Buddha statue standing 18 meters high and eight meters underground, totaling 26 meters. It is exquisitely molded, with mainly relief designs. For instance, wave designs are used in the carving of the clothing of the Bodhisattva (living Buddha), with clear and vigorous lines and highly striking embellishments.

The Ming and Qing dynasties (1368-1911) were a period in which woodcarving arts developed to its peak. Admirable small woodcarvings, practical utensils, decorative woodcarvings, along with delightful carved furnishings, all underwent great development. Woodcarving art was widely used in palatial and housing construction. Some famous woodcraftsmen and woodcarving genres from this period reflected different styles and schools of woodcarving art, such as Zhejiang's Dongyang woodcarving, Guangdong's Chaozhou gold-lacquer woodcarving, boxwood carving, and Fujian's Longyan woodcarving.

2. The Main Schools and Characteristics of Folk Woodcarvings

Owing to differences in customs, materials used and techniques in various places, China's folk woodcarving has formed several major schools, including Zhejiang's Dongyang woodcarving, Guangdong's Chaozhou gold-lacquer woodcarving, Fujian woodcarving, Jiangsu's Suzhou red-sandalwood and Leqing boxwood carving, Hebei's Chengde woodcarving, Shandong's Qufu and Yunnan's Jianchuan woodcarving.

Corbel in the shape of a dancing girl: Song Dynasty, Kaiyuan Monastery in Quanzhou City, Fujian Province

Below-eaves woodcarving:
Lu residence in Dongyang

Dongyang woodcarving

Zhejiang's Dongyang region has long been known as the "land of woodcarving design." Legend has it that Dongyang woodcarving originated in the Tang Dynasty. During the Southern Song Dynasty (1127-1279), Dongyang became one of the places where books printed with carved wooden blocks flourished the most. The earliest extant Dongyang wood-carved objects are the statues of a boy prodigy of the Song Dynasty and of the Goddess of Mercy (Avalokitesvara Bodhisattva), unearthed from the Nansi Temple Pagoda in Dongyang. In the Ming Dynasty (1368-1644), Dongyang woodcarving was mainly used in construction and for ornamentation. During the Qing Dynasty (1644-1911), Dongyang woodcarving was especially renowned for aspects such as carved wood furniture, daily-use articles and ornamental carved wooden utensils. Of the surviving relatively famous buildings in the region of Zhejiang, the wood-carved ornaments were mostly made by Dongyang craftsmen. The feature of Dongyang woodcarving is that it was able to adopt different decorative techniques according to the different types of architecture and furniture, through the simultaneous use of techniques of relief, alto-relivo, openwork carving, and three-dimensional carving. Openwork carving and three-dimensional carving were used for beams, pillars, tie-beam, brackets and consoles of buildings; shallow relief was used in lower part of the partition boards, bordered panels; openwork carving and three-dimensional carving were used for window divisions and balustrades; and the technique of three-dimensional carving was usually adopted for furnishings and artistic woodcarving. Dongyang woodcarving adopted wide-ranging subjects as motif, its carving work exquisite in molding and its painted work realistic. Of the extant architectural range of Dongyang woodcarvings, the Lu residence in Dongyang is the best preserved, with an imposing courtyard and superb woodcarvings.

Guangdong's Chaozhou gold-lacquer woodcarving

Chaozhou gold-lacquer woodcarving is so named because of its japanning (black gloss finish) and gilding after carving. During the Ming and Qing dynasties, the Chaozhou region's prosperous trade and solid economic base led to the extensive use of Chaozhou woodcarvings in construction and ornamentation. Guangdong gold-lacquer woodcarvings are divided into two major schools, Chaozhou and Guangzhou. The Chaozhou School, also known as "Chaozhou woodcarvings," became most developed in Chaozhou, Chao'an, Chaoyang, Puning, Chenghai, as well as other counties.

Interior room furnishings: Qingyuanshan, Weifang, Shandong Province

Chaozhou gold-lacquer woodcarvings were usually used in building, furniture, sacred implements and other ornamental architectural components. The themes of the carvings were taken mostly from folk legends, fairytales, drama or opera characters, as well as flowers, birds, insects and fish. Chaozhou woodcarvings combine both form and spirit, the carving work meticulously done, the picture composition full and symmetric, and the colors splendid, glittering with gold and jade, giving it unique features. Take the architectural woodcarvings of the Ma Zu Temple in Chaozhou for example. Its beautiful shape and its strong colors make people acclaim such works as the acme of perfection.

Partition boards: Lu residence in Dongyang

Introduction

Partition board with the pattern of
birds and beasts, Dongyang

Huizhou woodcarving

These are mostly found in trusses, brackets, eaves bars, railing panels, and window bars, as well as ornamental carvings on furniture. Generally, relief artwork is used in the core of the upper part of a partition board, apron boards (the lower part of a partition board) and bordered panels (the middle section of a partition board), its designs including drama and entertainment figures, and military skills contests; while three-dimensional carving art is used in bolsters and corbels, its designs including lions with embroidered balls, various kinds of flowers, birds, human figures, pavilions, terraces, halls, and auspicious designs. Its composition of images is full, its layers are rich, and carving work is fine, making them look very lifelike.

Boxwood carving

Its main places of production are Leqing and Wenzhou in Zhejiang Province. Its name comes from the use of boxwood as the carving material. Boxwood is taken from perennial evergreen trees, which grow extremely slow. The quality of boxwood is durable, its texture fine and detailed, and its color is slightly yellow, gradually darkening with the passing of time. It is a precious material for carving exquisite miniatures. Boxwood carvings consist mainly of small carved items, mostly ornamental articles placed on one's desk. The earliest evidence is the portrait of "Li, Iron Crutch," one of the Eight Immortals, from the Yuan Dynasty (1271-1368), which is kept in the Imperial Palace in Beijing. Boxwood carvings technically absorb the skills of stone carving and ivory carving. The work procedures include making rough base, meticulous carving, then waxing or varnishing. Its forms include single figure three-dimensional carving, composite carving, openwork carving and group carving. The carvings are mostly of Goddess of Mercy, arhats, female celestials, mischievous boys, galloping horses, as well as flowers, birds, fish and insects. Famous boxwood craftsmen include Wenzhou's folk master engraver Zhu Zichang (1876-1934), Wang Fengzuo, Wang Dufang, and the Yu brothers.

Fuzhou woodcarving

Wood-carved statues and shrines of deities have been popular since ancient times in the Fuzhou area, and later developed into architectural woodcarvings and ornamental wooden furniture components. During the Qing Dynasty, Fuzhou woodcarvings were divided into three schools – the Xiangyuan School, Daban School and Yanta School – after the village names. Tree-root carvings and longan-wood carvings carry distinctive local features among Fuzhou wooden carvings. In the late Ming Dynasty and early Qing Dynasty, the root carvings created by Kong Mou, a woodcarving master of Lianjiang, Fujian Province, were acclaimed, so folk artists vied with one another to imitate them, engaging in artistic creation by making use of various natural forms of tree roots, succeeding in creating this special category of tree-root carving. Longan woodcarvings rose in Daban Village during the Qing Dynasty, with local craftsmen skilled at carving arhats, Eight Immortals, Bodhisattva, female celestials, beautiful women, as well as animals.

Unicorn representing auspiciousness carved in the center of a partition board, Heavenly King Mansion in Nanjing

"Phoenix Flying through Peony Flowers" carved in the center of a partition board, Heavenly King Mansion in Nanjing

Lower parts of two partition boards, one carved with the motif of dragon, the other with phoenix, Longquan Monastery, Wutai Mountain, Shanxi Province

Suzhou mahogany wood carving

Suzhou mahogany woodcarving has a long history. It uses precious mahogany as its carving material. The carving is mostly used for furniture and wood-carved ornaments. Since the Ming Dynasty, the "Suzhou style" developed, featuring simple molds, firm and smooth lines, fine workmanship, and exquisitely wrought and brightly polished works. Suzhou mahogany woodcarvings are skilled in the use of openwork carving, three-dimensional carving, deep and shallow relief, inlaying, intaglio, as well as other methods, taking mountains and rivers, flowers and birds, melons and fruits, insects and fish as subjects. Suzhou mahogany woodcarvings are done by applying a variety of engraving methods.

3. Main Decorative Locations and Subject Range of Folk Architectural Woodcarvings

Each architectural component of China's residential buildings could be an independent ornamental item. Found throughout various types of main halls, wing rooms, arches over gateways, archways or bedrooms of especially young girls, woodcarving art is widely used on beams, columns, brackets, doors and windows, *gualuo* (defined on P.33), *queti* brackets (defined on P.39), upturned eaves, carved wood cantilevers, lintels, balustrades, incense-burner tables, bed frames, and other furniture and furnishings; while three-dimensional carving and openwork carving are mostly found on bolster and brackets. Layout and structure are skillful, with multi-layers, yet not untidy. Themes and subjects include immortals, legends, opera figures, lion and ball, pavilions, terraces, halls, as well as various kinds of birds, beasts and flowers. Varying and complex image composition is mostly adopted, with extremely fine workmanship. As for its working procedures, Chaozhou woodcarvings, for instance, usually adopt knife methods of tapping, holding, whittling and plying, to complete the chiseling of rough blocks, and then carving is completed through the techniques of intaglio, relief, three-dimensional carving and openwork carving.

Doors and windows of residences are important locations for woodcarving ornamentation in people's houses in southern China. Partition boards are also widely used on the walls of the two sides of a hall. Such boards and windows are

elegantly carved with various patterns. Different knife methods are adopted for carving, so the cutting work is exquisite, and designs are rich. The core on the upper part of each partition board is carved with various images, including folk legends, opera figures, landscapes, flowers, birds and beasts, and the 12 traditional zodiac animals representing year of birth. Lines are convoluted, rich with change, along with clear-cut themes, distinct gradations, and vivid molding. People can appreciate them from different angles, which generate different visual effects.

Taishi and Shaoshi corbel,
Shexian County, Chengcunjiang,
Anhui Province

The interior furnishings of people's houses, that is, articles displayed and set inside as interior decor, such as screens, scrolls inscribed with long-life wishes, backdrop screen (wall-type partition), *bishachu* (definition see below), as well as various types of furniture, play the role of separating interior spaces and a display of wood-carved artworks. The interior backdrop screen is often set in the rear of the central hall. Facing the door, it is composed mostly of lattice, or with carved designs. In the main halls of southern Anhui residences, as well as other parts of south of the Yangtze River, painting or portrait scrolls are generally hung on such screens, above which are horizontal inscribed boards, while on both sides are couplets. A long, narrow table or "Eight Immortals" table is set in front of such a exquisitely carved screen with classic mahogany armchairs arranged on its sides.

Bishachu, a kind of partition used indoors to separate space, is generally arranged in a direction to give depth. Eight or ten boards are adopted as one divider, two boards of which are used as an opening door. The partition door of the *bishachu* is composed mostly of lattice patterns where light can easily go through. Paper or thin yarn is used to cover the central part of the partition, which is decorated with calligraphic inscriptions or paintings. There are also solid wooden *bishachu* decorated with exquisite carvings, along with waxing

A carving under the eave of the Lu residence, Dongyang

in primary colors, also giving durability and visual effect.

Indoor furnishings include couplets written on scrolls and hung on hall pillars, horizontal inscribed boards and various types of small furnishings, including utensils for sacrificial ceremony, stools for potted flowers, latticed racks, wooden frames for calligraphy and painting, as well as things conneded with the

Openwork carvings with *Guizi* design of flowers and grasses

"scholar's four treasures" (writing brush, ink-stick, ink-slab and paper). All those are related to woodcarving.

Articles of furniture are practical items. There exists a wide variety of folk furniture, with carving as one of the main means for furniture ornamentation. Carving subjects include almost everything in the world.

The carved bed is one of the most complex style of artistic woodcarving in furniture, the wood-carved ornamentation on such beds mostly having relatively concentrated themes, including happy family, symbols of prosperity, high rank and longevity, a hundred birds paying homage to a phoenix, a unicorn sending the son, the Eight Immortals, the three topmost scholars in feudal society, fishing, woodcutting, plowing, as well as literary themes. Some carved beds contain series of illustrations following the plots of stories; such as in "beds featuring a unicorn sending the son," which contains such pictures as "a boy riding a unicorn," "mother expressing hopes for her child to have a bright future," "studying at a cold night" (signifying perseverance in one's studies despite hardships), "bringing glory to one's ancestors." The carving work is generally done using methods combining openwork carving and relief, and using the backdrop of shallow relief to set off the main object of deep relief. Various kinds of designs of flower and grass are used to combine and connect separate pictures and merge them into an organic whole, to make the carved bed more beautiful and colorful. In terms of the technical process, several wooden blocks are carved one by one through methods of relief or openwork carving; when this is finished, the blocks are assembled and the whole process is completed.

The four legs of rectangular tables, desks and tea tables are generally carved with dragons, phoenixes and lions. Often a lion is carved at the feet of each leg of a carefully designed table; and from the legs upward are engraved things such as "Two Dragons Jostling for a Pearl," or "Two Phoenixes Facing the Sun." The sides of such furniture are carved with flowers and grasses, full of flavors of life, and the carving is topped by lacquering and colorful drawings, making the furniture especially splendid.

Small wood-carved ornamentations on horizontal inscribed boards and couplets written on scrolls which hung on hall pillars, taking writings as motifs, are mostly written by famous people. The calligraphic level is superb, and connotations of the writings are deep, possessing a strong cultural flavor. Most of the inscribed boards are rectangular in shape, or in a hand-scroll shape, and boards of unique and unconventional shapes, such as banana-leaf boards painted green and hung on whitewashed walls, looking very elegant, called "banana-leaf in snow." Horizontal inscribed boards serving as name-boards or signboards of a shop were often used for commercial stores. Couplets written on scrolls and hung from hall pillars are mostly in vertical rectangular shape and engraved with poetry or prose. Inscribed boards in residences and gardens south of the Yangtze River were often engraved in mineral azure or mineral green, which look very elegant. The inscribed boards were mostly paired complementarily, which were generally hung over lintels or columns of buildings; while couplets were hung symmetrically on pillars on both sides. Inscribed boards and couplets would give a sense of beauty and unique character to buildings, effectively enhancing their aesthetic value and cultural elegance.

4. Decorative Motifs of Folk Architectural Woodcarvings

The decorative motifs for folk woodcarvings mostly demonstrate the inheritance of folk culture. This inheritance determines the universal use of formats, styles and standardization of folk artistic modeling. A set of complete and concise inherited methods, along with a technological system, is formed by which the masters pass their skills on to apprentices, presenting established styles, common to humankind yet different regionally. For example, the widely used decorative motifs loved by the people have applied traditional methods such as association, metaphor, comparison and homophones to transmit implied auspicious meanings. For example: using peach to represent long life, peony for wealth and rank, and pomegranate to signify many sons; using a goat to indicate filial piety, "Eight Concealed Immortals" to signify birthday congratulations; using plum, orchid, bamboo and chrysanthemum to mean moral integrity of gentlemen. Lotus is associated with honest and upright conduct. In the Chinese words "*bian fu*" (bat), "*fu*" sounds the same as "*fu*" (good fortune); while "*lu*" (deer) sounds the same as "rank"; "*ji*" (chicken) as "*ji*" (good luck), etc.

These typical auspicious decorative motifs are prominently expressed in Chinese folk architectural woodcarvings. Some folk building complexes displayed in this book, such as the Lu residence in Dongyang, Zhejiang Province, the Cai residence in Quanzhou, Fujian Province, as well as buildings in Suzhou gardens and Huizhou residences, are all outstanding representatives of Chinese folk architectural woodcarving arts. A

Woman warrior Hua Mulan: Dongyang woodcarving, from collection of Zhao Zhishuo glance over these folk architecture reveals the brilliant architectural woodcarving arts wholly displayed before us, with perfect craftsmanship, great dynamism, vivid form and clear-cut motifs, all making visitors marvel.

The decorative motifs of folk architectural woodcarvings can be summed up in three major categories: praying for good fortune and bringing good luck, ethical education, and exorcising evil and warding off disaster. Praying for good fortune and bringing good luck is the most extensively used theme in folk building decor, with people summing it up as fortune, rank, longevity, pleasure, and wealth. Its main contents include: enhancing fertility, prolonging and increasing longevity, bringing in wealth and accepting good fortune, and high official positions and riches. These subjects are closely connected with the daily life of ordinary people. In simple and plain language, they express people's concerns over the value of life, hopes for prosperity for their families, aspirations for affluent and happy lives, as well as seeking their own social status.

Ethical education, as the subject of greatest significance in education, in folk architectural decoration, is found mostly in motifs and forms of historical allusions, scenes of production and life, calligraphy and couplets, by which to praise the morality and integrity of being a good filial son or brother, being loyal and faithful, kindhearted and virtuous, making clear the hierarchy of human relationships, Confucian etiquette, circumstances evoking people's feelings of respecting the old and cherishing the young; as one is influenced by what one constantly hears and sees, cultivating oneself and having a good family. These decorative phenomena, which take the living environment as spiritual vehicles, are meant to exert subtle influences on people's moral character, thus intensifying the spiritual functions of buildings.

Exorcising evil spirits and warding off disaster, pursuing happiness and good health are main themes of concern to the common people, generation after generation. People often use auspicious pictures to decorate architectural components, with the intent of eliminating pestilence, suppressing evil spirits and warding off disaster, a role equal to magic incantations for eliminating disaster and averting misfortune.

The decorative designs found throughout folk architectural woodcarvings are all-embracing, and can be summed up as follows: auspicious fowls and lucky beasts, flowers and grasses, worship of deities, stories of human personages, utensils, patterns on brocade and symbolic written characters. Auspicious fowls and lucky beasts include the dragon, phoenix, unicorn, lion, tiger, deer, turtle, monkey, goat, rat, crane, chicken, egret, paradise flycatcher, mandarin duck, fish, and toad; while the flowers and grasses include peony, lotus, orchid, magnolia, Chinese crabapple, chrysanthemum, pine, bamboo, and plum. Deities include gods of good fortune, high position and longevity, the god of literature and the Eight Immortals; and stories of personages mostly draw their material from famous classical works such as *Creation of the Gods, Romance of the Three Kingdoms* and *Journey to the West*; dramas like *Generals of the Yang Family, Birthday Congratulations from Guo Ziyi*, as well as fairytales such as *The Legend of White Snake, Liu Hai Playing with a Golden Toad*. Utensils include "Eight Concealed Immortals," being the immortals' ritual implements: the fan, treasure sword, jade flute, treasure bottle-gourd, jade tablet, percussion instrument, basket of flowers, and lotus flowers, eight good fortunes (Buddhist ritual implements: lotus flowers, treasure bottle, fish, tray, wheel of Dharma, triton, treasure umbrella, and white canopy), miscellaneous treasures (combination of things such as jewels, ancient coins, square-shaped ornamental objects for women, jade percussion instruments, articles made of rhinoceros horns, silver ingots, S-shaped ornamental objects, coral, auspicious clouds, folium *artemisiae argyi*, ancient cooking vessels, calligraphy and painting); geometric motifs include repetitive patterns such as clouds, thunder, ice crackle, fret, Buddhist swastika, and turtleback; auspicious writing includes such designs as those using "*fu*" (good fortune), "*shou*" (long life), as well as swastika, Sanskrit and Arabic words.

"Lin Daiyu Burying Flowers" (scene
from classic novel *A Dream of Red
Mansions*): Dongyang woodcarving,
from collection of Zhao Zhishuo

ARCHITECTURAL
COMPONENTS

Architectural Components

Truss

Trusses in folk buildings not only have significance in terms of structural functions, but also abound in beauty in their structure and ornamentation. A truss is composed mainly of pillars, beams and tie beams. Each component has particular decorative forms. Trusses in folk buildings are often used in a way that one side of them can be seen from the outside, which are rather decorative. They are either plain or covered with colorful paintings or carvings. The plain ones can fully demonstrate the quality of the wood and the original structural beauty.

A beam is a horizontal timber supported by pillars or other frames. Its cross section revealed to the outside is basically rectangular in shape, with many modeling changes on this basis, forming a variety of beam designs.

A square-shaped tie beam is a timber set on top of a pillar and between *queti* brackets and other brackets, as a type of wooden component used to keep level and connect various truss members. Tie beams are key locations for decorations below eaves, while decorated tie beams between peripheral columns are often applied with color painting or sculpture, the protruding part in the pattern of "fist-shaped beam heads."

▶ Woodcarving on a beam frame, Lu residence in Dongyang

Below-eaves corbel, Lu residence in Dongyang

22

An arch ceiling bracket, Lu residence in Dongyang

Arch ceiling brackets, Lu residence in Dongyang

Happiness Appearing on the Eyebrows

The picture, also named "Magpie Flying up the Plum Tree," and "Magpie Forecasting the Coming of Spring," shows a pair of magpies perched on a plum branch. Since people consider magpies to be a happy omen, and in Chinese "plum" and "eyebrow" sound the same (*mei*), the picture "Happiness Appearing on the Eyebrows" symbolizes an approaching happy event.

Mandarin Ducks Playing amony Lotus Flowers

Female and male mandarin ducks are inseparable as the body and its shadow. The folk proverb, "Admiring only mandarin ducks and not celestial beings," mostly signifies husband and wife getting along peacefully in devoted love.

A truss member carved with
"Mandarin Ducks Playing among Lotus Flowers", and "Happiness Appearing on the Eyebrows", Liang Garden in Foshan, Guangdong Province

A truss member carved with
"Phoenix and Unicorn Facing the Sun", Liang Garden in Foshan

Architectural Components

A truss member carved with "A Carp Leaping into the Dragon Gate",
Liang Garden in Foshan, Guangdong

An arch ceiling entitled "Living Peacefully in All Seasons",
Keyuan Garden in Chaozhou, Guangdong Province

Design of a pair of lions, detail of an arch ceiling component, Nanhua Youlu in Chaozhou

Chaozhou Gold-lacquer Woodcarvings

"Chaozhou gold-lacquer woodcarving" derived its name through the lacquering and gilding techniques applied after carving. Guangdong's gold-lacquer woodcarving is divided into two major schools of Chaozhou and Guangzhou. Chaozhou gold-lacquer woodcarving is most developed in counties such as Chao'an, Chaoyang, Puning and Chenghai. Chaozhou gold-lacquer woodcarving is usually utilized in buildings, furniture and sacred implements as adornment or components. The carving motifs mostly have materials drawn from folklore, fairytales, drama characters, as well as flowers, birds, insects and fish. It combines form and spirit, and is carved with great care, the picture composition full and symmetric, its color splendid and magnificent, all with distinct features.

28

Figures, gold-lacquer woodcarving, Ma Zu Temple in Chaozhou

Gold-lacquer woodcarving with the motif of a deer,
Dongshan Guan Yu Temple in Zhangzhou

Deer

Chinese people honor deer as an auspicious creature. The Chinese word for "deer" (*lu*) is homophonic with "high rank," therefore, deer have become the symbol of high-ranking position. And it is the auspicious symbol for those seeking high position. The ancients took white deer as the most precious, as a reference to the mount of celestial beings, also implying long life. Models of deer are mostly in the posture of turning their heads.

Gold-lacquer woodcarving with the motif of a lion,
Dongshan Guan Yu Temple in Zhangzhou, Fujian Province

Gold-lacquer woodcarving with figures,
Dongshan God Guan Yu Temple in Zhangzhou

Hanging Column

Located at the festoon gate and beneath the eaves, it is a kind of short column that does not reach the ground. The top of the hanging column in popular architecture assumes the form of simple square corners, hexagonal or octagonal. In the floral arch gates of ancestral temples, guild halls, as well as *siheyuan* (traditional residential compound with houses around a courtyard) or courtyard houses in Beijing, the forms of the hanging columns are varied and colorful, complexly layered, with refined carving workmanship, appearing in the forms of bottle-gourds, baskets and palace lanterns.

Lotus Design

In the Spring and Autumn and Warring States periods, it was used for decorative carving. After Buddhism was introduced into China, the lotus has often been used as a symbol of Buddhism, representing Sukhavati (Pure Land), and symbolizing purity and virtue and implying good fortune.

Guaizi design from a truss,
Cai residence in Quanzhou, Fujian

Lotus, Dongshan Guan Yu
Temple in Zhangzhou

Bracket

It is a wooden angle-shaped support formed by tenon and mortise structure. Brackets can be complemented by colorful paintings and sculptures, intensifying the sense of beauty. In feudal society, such bracket was a symbol of honor, respect and rank, and was not allowed to be used in dwellings of ordinary people, but could only be seen in certain monasteries or large public buildings.

Brackets

Gualuo

Gualuo is an embellishment found under decorative tie beams between gallery columns. *Gualuo* can be made with wooden lattices, or made of a whole board with carvings. If the two ends of the *gualuo* are very drooping, it becomes a hanging openwork screen. Generally, *gualuo* is exquisite, with decorations of dragon, phoenix, magpie, plum, vines and branches.

Figures and auspicious creatures on a *gualuo*, Xiangfending Village, Shanxi Province

Figures in entwined branches on a *gualuo*, Shanxi-Shaanxi guild hall

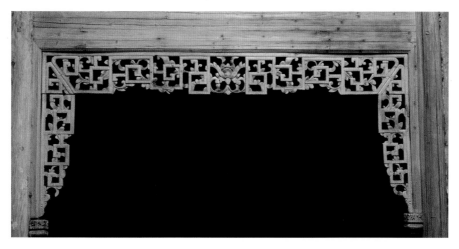

Guaizi design of a *gualuo*, Hongcun Village, Yixian County

Bogu and *Guaizi* designs of a *gualuo*, Qinghui Park in Shunde, Guangdong

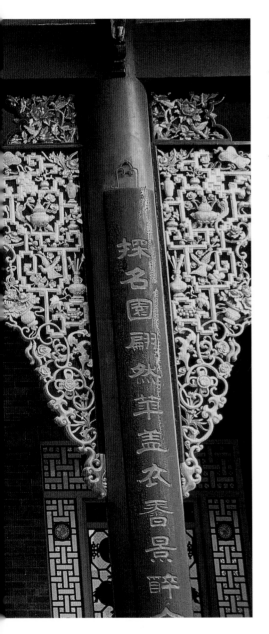

Bogu Design

Bogu designs are composed of images of copper stoves, ceramic vases, S-shaped ornamental wands, ancient gold percussion instruments, books, calligraphy and paintings, and sometimes decorated and embellished with flowers and fruit. In the Northern Song Dynasty (960-1127), when the practice of resurrecting the ancient culture was in vogue, Emperor Hui Zong (1082-1135) ordered Minister Wang Fu and others to classify ancient objects kept in Xuanhe Hall and compile a 30-volume book titled *Xuanhe Bogu Pictures.* Later generations referred to the designs of such ancient objects as "*Bogu* Design," conveying a meaning of upholding study and refinement; so they are often used in décor for scholarly families or families producing public officials for several generations.

Architectural Components

Balustrade

Wooden balustrades are set between columns, as structural components used for support, or protective barriers, as well as for resting and leaning upon. Balustrades are often seen in people's residences. The wooden balustrade has a variety of forms, for instance, there are balustrades installed along the edge of one side of the corridor on each floor of a storied house, balustrades on the flat roofs of storehouses, hand banisters installed between stairs, seat or seat-back balustrades installed beneath gallery eaves, and wall-type balustrades beneath windows. Wooden balustrades are mostly composed of lattices and complemented with decorative carvings, forming elegant designs with easy passage of light. There are many fine balustrade types found in the gardens of southern China, particularly those beneath pavilions, terraced pavilions and galleries. They are useful for leaning upon to enjoy the landscape, along with their decorative function.

The top of a baluster column,
Zhuozheng Garden in Suzhou,
Jiangsu Province

Balustrade woodcarving, the Cheng residence in Tunxi, Anhui

Balustrade woodcarving, Cao residence, Shanxi Province

Balustrade woodcarving, Cao residence, Shanxi Province

Queti Bracket

This is a wooden component for bolstering beam and tie beam at a joining point. The *queti* brackets in traditional Chinese buildings have a variety of representative forms. In the small spanning space between two pillars, two *queti* brackets may link to each other and serve as butt joints. There are sometimes full-length *queti* brackets on both sides of a pillar, or elegant *queti* brackets beneath the roof of porches of residences, or between beams and tie beams. *Queti* brackets can often soften the rigid angles between beams and tie beams, also containing carvings, paintings and other superb artistic adornments, giving it very high artistic value.

Horse-shoe-shaped bracket carved with birds and animals,
Cai residence in Quanzhou

Horse-shoe-shaped bracket carved with fish and algae,
Dongshan Guan Yu Temple in Zhangzhou

Architectural Components

Qieti bracket with design of auspicious animals and birds, Cai residence in Quanzhou

Qieti bracket with design of auspicious animals and birds, Cai residence in Quanzhou

Corbel

This is located on the outer side of the peripheral column, angled to support the wooden components under the projecting eaves, purlins and tie beams. Corbels are simply structured and adroit, making a very effective structural form. A corbel is generally called a "strutting arch," especially those that have a square block which is thick and heavy. Corbels are covered with many types of decoration. Its subjects are rich, and its motifs include dragons, phoenixes, flowers and birds, as well as human figures. Particularly in the residences of Zhejiang's Dongyang and Anhui's Hui schools, corbels' superb carvings, lifelike figures and images of animals are acclaimed as the acme of perfection.

Corbels with human figures, Dingxiang Memorial Hall of Dongyang, Zhejiang

Carved work on truss

"A Pair of Lions Playing with a Ball":
corbel, Lu residence in Dongyang

Carved work on truss

A Child on a Lion's Back Entering the Gate

The following two pictures show a child riding on a lion's back; the lion, a silk embroidered ball in its paw, is followed by a small lion on one side. Lions are considered auspicious animals; and a child riding on a lion's back bodes good fortune, high position and other happy events for the family.

Lion and child, corbels, Lu residence in Dongyang

God of Blessing, corbels, Shexian County, Anhui

God of Blessing

Ranking first of three deities, God of Heaven specializes in blessings. The "three deities" refer to the gods of "heaven, earth and water" in Taoism. It is said that the god of Heaven is in charge of blessings, the god of Earth oversees pardons, and that of Water alleviates adversity. People worship them as the "Three Supreme Beings."

He-He Celestial Beings

The two celestial beings known as "He-He" (literally peace and harmony) are each mostly seen in the image of a child, one holding a lotus flower, the other holding a round box, implying harmony and good relations. Legend has it that the two celestials – Hanshan and Shide – were two men dear to each other as brothers, who loved the same girl, without being aware of the other's feelings. It was only just before marriage that Hanshan learned the truth, so he abandoned his home to go to Suzhou's Fengqiao, where he shaved his head and became a monk. On learning this, Shide also gave up the girl and went to Fengqiao, where the two men were overjoyed to see each other as monks, and built the Hanshan Temple on a mountain. The two celestials of He-He are honored as auspicious gods. During wedding ceremonies in ancient times their portraits were often hung in the hall of the residence of the new couple.

Liu Hai Scattering Coins

Liu Hai was a famous Chinese Taoist priest living in the period of the 10th century. Usually a picture of Liu Hai looks like this: Liu Hai, with a string of coins in hand, dancing with a golden toad. It is said that Liu Hai often scattered coins to make people wealthy. A folk rhyme goes: "Liu Hai plays with a golden toad, scattering coins with each step." The toad, similar to a frog, has three legs. People look upon the toad as a spirit. "Liu Hai scatters coins" implies good fortune and great wealth.

"Liu Hai Scattering Coins": corbel,
Cheng residence in Tunxi, Anhui

One of the two celestial beings
He-He, corbel, Hongcun Village in Yixian
County, Anhui

These are names of two ancient official positions. Taishi originally was the supreme commander of the army; while Shaoshi was an official tutoring the crown prince. The pronunciation of Da (large) Shi, Xiao (small) Shi are similar to that of Taishi and Shaoshi. Stone lions (*shi*) were customarily set up opposite each other in front of the gate of an official residence: with the left side of the gate representing "Taishi," one of the highest official ranks in the imperial court; while the right representing the young imperial tutor. Thus Taishi and Shaoshi symbolize achieving promotion step by step through a successful official career. The design expresses the good wishes that the official's families can pass on from generation to generation. A lion is considered the king among a hundred beasts, and also seen as a supernatural creature in Buddhism, symbolizing sacredness and auspiciousness. A lion also indicates official rank and powerful status. Gate lions guard the house in a display of dignity and auspiciousness, as symbols of dispelling evil spirits, and of wealth and power.

Taishi and Shaoshi: corbel,
Shexian County, Anhui

Lion and embroidered ball:
corbel, Shexian County

Lion and embroidered ball,
corbel, Hongcun Village, Anhui

Taishi and Shaoshi,
corbel, Wuyuanxu Village,
Jiangxi Province

Lions and Silk Embroidered Ball

This design is composed of lions and a silk embroidered ball. The lion is considered the king among a hundred beasts, ferocious and dignified. People believe the lion is capable of exorcising evil spirits and guarding the home. A silk embroidered ball is seen as propitious. A design using such a ball as the motif is known as "embroidered ball." "*Shi* (lion)" is homophonic with "*shi*" (master) and "*qiu*" (ball) with "*qiu*" (seeking), so "lions and embroidered ball" symbolize official rank and high status. There is also another tale about a male lion and a female lion playing together: the lions' fur becomes tangled together and rolls into a ball, giving birth to a baby lion; thus symbolizing multiplying of future generations and prosperity for the family. "Lions and embroidered ball" also evolved into "lion dances," transmitting good omens for fortune and jubilation, and becoming an enduring folk custom activity.

Long-life crane, corbel, Lu residence in Dongyang

Living as Long as Pines and Cranes

This is also known as "Pines and Cranes All Enjoy Long Life" and "Pines and Cranes Always Look Young." The pine is an evergreen tree, while the crane is a bird of longevity. Pictures composed of cranes and pines imply permanent youthfulness, longevity and happiness.

A Phoenix Flying through Peony Flowers

This is also known as "The Phoenix Loves Peonies" and "The Peony Attracts Phoenixes." The phoenix is a propitious bird of legend. The peony is also considered a flourishing flower, the king among all flowers, signifying riches, auspiciousness and beauty. "A Phoenix Flying through Peony Flowers" implies that the phoenix would bring auspiciousness and wealth.

"A Phoenix Flying through Peony Flowers":
corbel, Lu residence in Dongyang

Deer design, corbel, Lu residence in Dongyang

DOOR AND WINDOW
COMPONENTS

Door and Window Components

Partition Board
It is a wood-carved board functioning as a partition placed inside a hall; the upper part of such a board is generally installed with latticework, or covered with paper or glass.

Spring in All Four Seasons
The four pictures of spring, summer, autumn and winter composed of flowers from the four seasons, such as narcissus, lotus, chrysanthemum and plum, together with birds, signify the continuation of spring through all four seasons, or perfect bliss and happiness.

Core of partition board, featuring "Spring in All Four Seasons"

Partition boards featuring "Spring in All Four Seasons",
residence in Yunnan's Lijiang Prefecture

Partition Door

Partition doors are formed as frames by grouping stiles and rails together, the central part of the upper part is generally called the "core" of the partition; the lower half of the partition board is large in area, referred to the "apron board." Sandwiched between the upper part and the apron board is a smaller, long horizontal section called the "boardered panel." The partition core is the key ornamental section, and should have very good light-admitting properties, with work as fine as possible to make it delicate and graceful, yet diffuse. Core designers often adopt decorative skills of carving, inlaying and finials.

Partition-board woodcarving, Hongcun Village in Yixian County

"Joyful News": the core of a
partition board, residence in Chengdu

Guaizi design, partition-board core

Partition-board woodcarving,
Lu residence in Dongyang

Phoenix Design

The phoenix is an auspicious bird in ancient folklore, gradually turning into a female symbol after the Han Dynasty (206 BC-AD 220). Phoenix designs are mostly used as adornment on folk robes or for wedding ceremonies.

Guaizi Design

In ancient China, the dragon was the symbol of imperial power. The emperor claimed himself as the "son of dragon." Except in temples and monasteries, where dragon designs could be used for decoration, people were not allowed to use it. Dragon designs were allowed to be used only for the robes of the royal family and as building ornamentation in the imperial palace.

Thus folk artists changed the form of dragon, and created the "*guaizi* (coil) design."

Guaizi designs are composed of dragon heads or crisscrossing and coiling geometrical or curling designs. Because "*guai*" and "*gui*" are pronounced almost the same, "*guai zi*" represents "*gui zi*", implying the flourishing of children and grandchildren, as well as serenity, wealth and rank.

Phoenix, *guaizi* design, apron board, Guanghua Monastery, on Wutai Mountain

Dragon-design apron board, Guanghua Monastery, on Wutai Mountain

Bogu design, apron board, the Chen clan ancestral temple in Guangzhou

Four seasons' flowers design, apron board, Chengdu Nunnery

Bogu Design

For details, see "*bogu* design" in "Architectural Components."

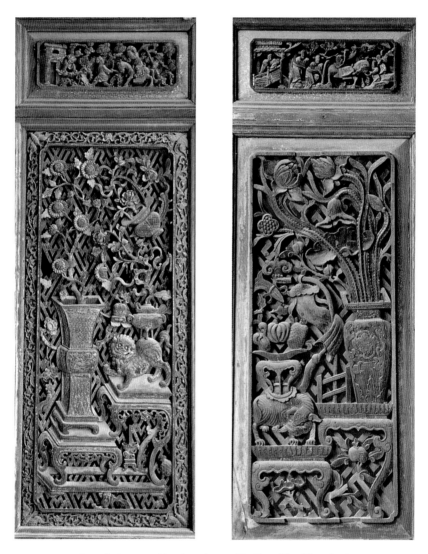

Bogu designs, partition-board core, Wu Feng (Five Phoenixes)
Building in Yongding County, Fujian

Bogu design, partition-board core,
Yuming Hall in Tianjin

"Prosperity and Peace":
partition-board core,
Yuming Hall in Tianjin

Two partition-board cores with flower-and-bird and 卐 designs, Yuming Hall in Tianjin

Figure designs, bordered panel, Cai residence in Quanzhou

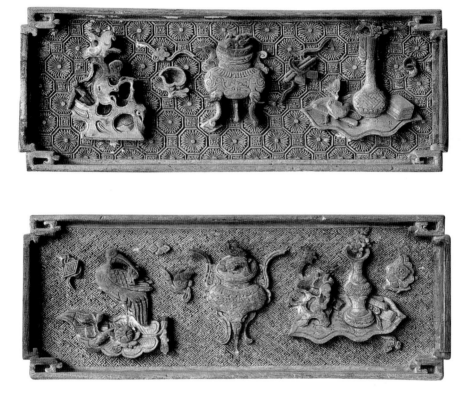

Two bordered panels with *bogu* design

Four bordered panels with various designs

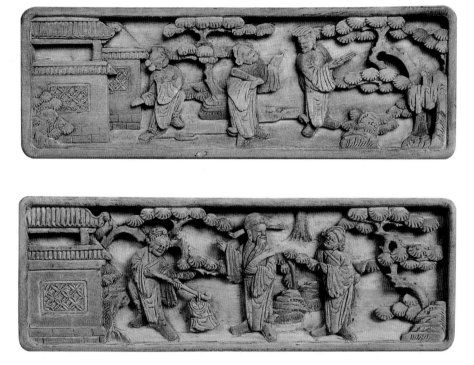

Figure designs, bordered panels, Zhuozheng Garden in Suzhou

"Auspicious Birds and Beasts": bordered panels,
Hongcun Village in Yixian County

Bogu designs, bordered panels, Jingxian County, Anhui

Door and Window Components

Bogu design, bordered panel, Lu residence in Dongyang

"Auspicious Birds and Beasts": bordered panel,
Lu residence in Dongyang

Bordered panel with *bogu* design

Bordered panel with auspicious animals, Lu residence, Dongyang

"Enjoying Lotus": bordered panel, Lu residence in Dongyang

Flower-and-bird design, bordered panel, Kaiyuan Monastery in Quanzhou

"A Cowherd Pointing to Apricot Flower Village (wine shop)":
bordered panel

Flower-and-bird design, bordered panel, Kaiyuan Monastery in Quanzhou

Er Jia Chuan Lu

This design is composed of crabs and reeds. In ancient times if one passed the *jia ke* (*jia* means "first" or "shell" in Chinese), or first class, in the imperial examination (the first round), and if one's name was at the end of the list, it was written on yellow (*huang*) paper, hence it was called "*huang jia.*" After the examination in the imperial court, the names of the successful candidates were announced, and the first one at this second round (*er* refers to this second round) was called "*chuan lu.*" Two big crabs mean "two shells," and "*lu,*" or reed, sounds the same as "list"; thus "*Er jia chuan lu*" means "passing the imperial examination."

"Er Jia Chuan Lu": bordered panel, Luzhou, Sichuan

"Eight Concealed Immortals": bordered panel, Luzhou, Sichuan

Eight Concealed Immortals

The Eight Immortals hold eight treasures in their hands, which are known as the "Eight Concealed Immortals": Han Zhongli's banana-leaf fan, Zhang Guolao's bamboo percussion instrument, Han Xiangzi's jade flute, Li Tieguai's treasure bottle-gourd, Lü Dongbin's treasure sword, Cao Guojiu's jade tablet, Lan Caihe's basket of flowers, and He Xiangu's lotus. It is said that the Eight Immortals' treasures each have certain supernatural powers, so people often utilize the "Eight Concealed Immortals" as amulets, praying to them for blessing and protection.

Cowherds, bordered panel, Lu residence in Dongyang

A fisherman, bordered panel, Lu residence in Dongyang

Bordered panels with designs of Eight Concealed Immortals,
flowers and bird, Lu residence in Dongyang

Bordered panels with designs of Eight Concealed Immortals,
flowers and bird, Lu residence in Dongyang

12 Zodiac Animals

China's earliest way of numbering calendar years was to use 12 animals to represent the 12 Earthly Branches, which are also known as the 12 zodiac animals. *Zi* is the rat; *chou* is the ox; *yin* is the tiger; *mao* is the rabbit; *chen* is the dragon; *ji* is the snake; *wu* is the horse; *wei* is the sheep; *shen* is the monkey; *you* is the chicken; *xu* is the dog; and *hai* is the pig. Because *Ganzhi* (combination of Heavenly Stems and Earthly Branches) is used to number the years, so the year in which a person is born is thus symbolized by a specific animal. People say that 12 zodiac animals can bring people auspiciousness, wealth, rank and peace.

Year of the Pig

Year of the Tiger

Squirrels and Grapes

Grape vines are laden with fruit, so it is compared to having multiple sons.

Squirrel is a variant of the rat, and the corresponding "Branch" position is "zi" in the 12 Earthly Branches, so there is the saying that, "The rat is the zi deity." The integration of the zi deity and fruitful grapes signify fertility and the wish for heirs, metaphorically meaning having many sons and grandsons.

"Squirrels and Grapes":
bordered panels, Sikouyan Village in Wuyuan County, Jiangxi

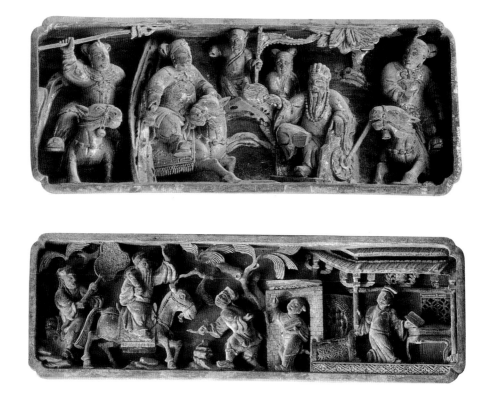

Figure design, bordered panels, Cai residence in Quanzhou

Flower-and-bird design, bordered panels,
Cai residence in Quanzhou

Longevity Character

The character for "longevity" or *shou* contains several variants in form; the long, thin one is known as "long life," while the round one is called "circular longevity." The varied characters of longevity have special auspicious implications. The combination of the seal character "*shou*" and the character of "卐" signifies "a 10,000 years of life."

Ancient Interlocking Coin Design

As a traditional architectural design, it resembles a string of copper cash with one ring interlocking with another, widely used in the designs of doors and windows.

Ancient interlocking coins and *guaizi* design, Kaiyuan Monastery in Quanzhou

Window Lattice

This refers to latticework made of interlocked battens or iron bars.

卐 Character

The character "卐" is pronounced "*wan*" (10,000); and the design formed continuously by this character is known as "*Wanhua Zhen*" (array of 10,000 flowers). It is a type of ancient talisman, and an auspicious symbol of Buddhism, implying eternal auspiciousness.

Happiness Character

The character for "happiness" (囍) is an auspicious symbol indispensable for weddings, being composed of the two words "*xi* (喜) and *xi* (喜) " and read as "*shuang xi*" (double happiness). Sometimes it signifies good luck, auspiciousness and celebration of a happy event. The pattern formed by two characters of "*xi*" is commonly called a "double happiness flower," used mostly for congratulations on a new marriage.

Window lattice with longevity character design

Window lattice with happiness character design

Bogu and *guaizi* designs, partion board, Jingxian County, Anhui

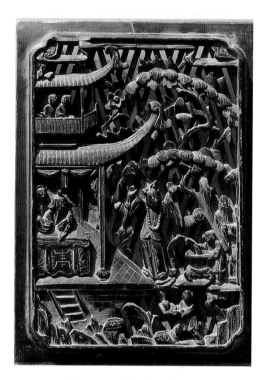

Figures, partition-board core,
Liang Garden in Foshan, Guangdong

"Impending Good Fortune and
Longevity": core of a partition board,
Yuming Hall in Tianjin

Longevity character design, window lattice,
Hongcun Village in Yixian County

Window lattice marked by the character of *"fu"* (good fortune),
western Hunan Province

Window lattice marked by the character of *"fu"* (good fortune),
western Hunan Province

Window rails, Cheng residence in Tunxi, Anhui

Two window balustrade woodcarvings with human figures,
Zuozheng Garden, Suzhou

Window balustrade carved with animals, Cai residence, Quanzhou

Five Bats Flying around Longevity Character

This is also called, "Five Blessings Descending upon One's Home." The picture is composed of five bats flying and dancing around the character "longevity", implying both good fortune and longevity. In Chinese eyes, the bat is a propitious animal, because its pronunciation is the same as that of "fortune" in Chinese, so the bat designs symbolize good fortune. The ancients were of the opinion that the perfect state of fortune should include five elements, namely, long life, many children, wealth,

"Five Bats Flying around Longevity Character": window rail, Dousan Street in Shexian County

virtue, and a good death; also known as the "five blessings." Chinese people often use "Five Bats Flying around Longevity Character" as a design for congratulating elders on birthdays. Sometimes the image is composed of five bats circling around the character "longevity," known as "good fortune and longevity lasting throughout the ages." "Five Bats Flying around Longevity Character" is one of the most common birthday congratulation designs used in Chinese society.

Door and Window Components

Bogu and *guaizi* design, window rails, Lu residence in Dongyang

Wealth, Rank and Auspiciousness

It is a pattern composed of a rooster and peony. In Chinese, the word for "chicken" (*ji*) is homophonic with "auspiciousness," while the peony symbolizes wealth and rank. The rooster is said to be a bird sent by the heavenly god, responsible for bringing happiness to the human world. Ancient people believed that chickens had five virtues – being well versed in literature and in military affairs, bravery, benevolence, and good faith. It is considered an auspicious bird, which eats the five poisonous things, suppresses evil and eliminates evil spirits. People worship the rooster as a talisman that ghosts and goblins fear the most.

Window rail carved with rooster and peony,
Youshan Village in Wuyuan County, Shanxi

Flower-grass design, window rail woodcarving,
Youshan Village in Wuyuan County, Shanxi

FURNISHINGS AND FURNITURE

Furnishings and Furniture

Couplets

Couplets written on scrolls and hung on
the pillars of halls, a practice continu-
ing to this day, are generally referred to
as "couplets."

One piece of the couplets, openwork,
Yuming Hall in Tianjin

Two kinds of couplets written on scrolls
and hung on hall pillars,
Hongguan in Wuyuan County, Jiangxi

"Lao Zi Leaves Hanguguan Pass":
hanging woodcarving, Qinghui Garden in Shunde, Guangdong

Lao Zi Leaves Hanguguan Pass

This describes a scene of westward travel by Lao Zi (571-471 BC), a great ancient Chinese philosopher who rode a green ox, advancing on the "Purple Air." It is said that Governor Yin Xi, of Hanguguan Pass, was fond of observing constellations, and one day discovered a divine star passing the Pleiades during its westward travel. He also saw "Purple Air" from the east advancing westward like a dragon and snake, so he forecast that there would be a sage going westward through Hanguguan. Soon afterward, Lao Zi came riding a black ox, so Yin Xi went out of Hanguguan Pass to greet him and ask him to be his teacher. Lao Zi stayed at Hanguguan Pass for a couple of days, propagated doctrines and gave his student a volume known as *The Book of Dao and Its Virtue* (*Dao De Jing*) to be handed down to future generations. People believed that "Lao Zi Leaves Hanguguan Pass" was a good omen, forecasting sages would descend upon the world.

Figure design,
hanging woodcarvings

Taishi Wall

This refers to the wall-type partition set up in the rear part of the hall, right opposite the door of the house. Latticework is most often used while carved designs are used as decoration. Taishi Walls inside main halls of residences of people south of the Yangtze River and in Fujian Province are often carved with designs for good fortune and longevity.

Four pictures carved on the Taishi Wall, Guozhuang Village, Hangzhou

Wood-carved Furniture

Household furniture consist of many varieties, classified in accordance with functions of usage in six major categories, namely, seating, beds, containers, chests or cabinets, frames, and screens. Luxurious pieces of furniture are made of hardwood, such as *huanghuali* wood (*Dalbergia odorifera T.Chen*), red sandalwood and chicken wing wood. Generally, sets of household furniture are made of such wood as elm, oak and beech cypress. Traditional household furniture makes full use of timber quality attributes of the material itself, trying as far as possible to display the charm of its natural grain. Different decorative techniques are applied in accordance with the structural characteristics of various components, so the decorative craftsmanship is extremely rich. Carving is one of the main measures utilized for embellishing the furniture. The techniques include line engraving, relief, openwork carving, and three-dimensional carving. Carving ornamentation is all-inclusive, with figures, animals, flowers, grasses and auspicious characters.

"Unicorn Sending the Son": furniture, Tianjin

◀ "Blessings and Longevity": Taishi Wall, Cai residence in Quanzhou

Carved wardrobe, Lu residence in Dongyang

Taishi Armchair

It is a kind of large traditional wooden
chair with a back and arms.

Lotus design, Taishi armchair,
collection of Huang Dianqi, Tianjin

Dragon-design table, collection of
Zheng Wantao, Suzhou

Carved table, the Huo ancestral temple in Foshan

Three Stars Shining Bright

It is composed of three celestial beings, namely, the Star of Fortune, the Star of Rank, and the Star of Longevity. It is said that they respectively oversee fortune, rank and longevity. The Star of Fortune looks after misfortune and fortune; the Star of Rank oversees the rich and honorable as well as the poor and lowly; and the Star of Longevity deals with life and death. The design implies that the three stars shine on the house, so the whole family enjoys happiness, affluence and long life.

"Three Stars Shining Bright": basin stand detail, western Hunan Province

Unicorn-design basin stand,
Beijing Folk Culture Park

"Unicorn Sending A Son":
basin stand, Beijing Folk Culture Park

Basin stand for opera performer

Furnishings and Furniture

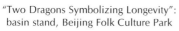

"Two Dragons Symbolizing Longevity":
basin stand, Beijing Folk Culture Park

Babu Bed

This is a huge bed looking like a wooden house. Apart from the bed, it has a ceiling and a space in front of the bed, which can be used to place small chairs, a cabinet, and other daily-use articles. The bed has a floor on which the house-like frame is set up. It is consisted of carved eaves, boards on both sides and the back. The front board of the bed is of fine workmanship, usually with a central motif, such as the "Two Celestials He-He," "The Unicorn Sending A Son," or opera stories. A number of board designs, centered round the same theme, are carved with different scenes and patterns, which form independent pictures with a sense of holistic harmony.

In light of its different qualities of timber and carving workmanship, the *babu* bed can be divided into hardwood *babu* bed or gold-lacquer wood-carved *babu* bed. The size and workmanship of *babu* beds vary based on the social status of the users.

Babu bed

Eight *babu* bed front boards carved with opera characters

Folk Woodcarving

Detail of the photo on P.115

德　姻舅生有至性紉即通方其在就傳之
年已冠之望乃年甫弱冠嚴君見背因
慨然曰母氏勞苦當盡承顏先業式徵遺言
鼓舞於是暫權鬻貨更薰力田初不屑屑於

謹序

茲之戲燕詞而稱祝者盡為眉壽之嘖矣云
德彰彰如此行見膺介福錫遐齡正未有艾
預卜門楣之光也夫觀　姻舅與孺人之至

Screen inscribed with
longevity wishes,
Liang Garden, Foshan

恭祝

皇上五代同堂推恩海內
天語煌煌錫以熙朝人瑞諸君子謀製屏以誌美吾父
又不以為安而辭之今吾母年八旬矣儷數一言
以壽母且以見吾父生平樂賢之志有助云爾余

大慈範尊四伯祖母吳氏老孺人八旬加一榮壽
蓋聞嘉耦兆萬福之原地道者有終之義余于
孺人之徽範而佐吾　先德伯祖

八回順卩華瑤邑

吕琹棟耸數錦屏

Screen inscribed with longevity wishes, Liang Garden, Foshan

Figure-design,
partition-board cores, Lu residence in Dongyang

Bringing Wealth and Treasure

This is a design composed of four written characters (*zhao cai jin bao*), an auspicious term mostly used by merchants doing business. Similar to this design are "Five Gods of Wealth" and "A Boy Brings in Wealth," usually composed of the god of wealth, a boy and a shoe-shaped gold or silver ingot. It implies flourishing sources of wealth and business.

"Bringing Wealth and Treasures": carved screen,
Liu residence in Dayi County, Chengdu City

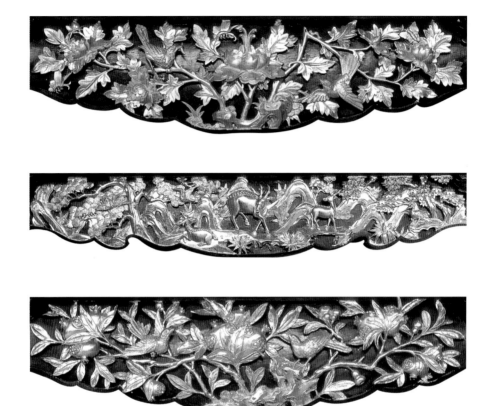

Three pictures from a long, narrow table board,
Huo clan ancestral temple in Foshan

Long, Narrow Table

It is a type of long, narrow table, specifically, measuring over 3 meters long and about 0.5 meter wide, on which various utensils and other articles are placed.

Minor Artworks (*Xiaopin*)

Originally *Xiaopin* referred to the abridged edition of Buddhist scriptures, and later extended to mean short essays or other short forms of presentation; here it refers to minor artworks.

A pair of lions, collection of Wang Jinhua

"Taishi and Shaoshi": collection of Wang Jinhua

"Taishi and Shaoshi":
Chen family ancestral temple in Guangzhou

TRADITIONAL FOLK
IMPLEMENTS

Traditional Folk Implements

Nuo Drama Mask

"*Nuo* drama mask" is short for "Nuotang drama mask," used in Guizhou Province for keeping away pestilence. It has circulated mainly among the Tujia, Miao and Bouyei peoples in Guizhou, as well as the Han. *Nuo* drama has strong religious color, its performance staged invariably together with such traditional folk activities as exorcising evil spirits and praying for good fortune. *Nuo* drama masks are made mostly with willow or white poplar wood, since willow wood is widely believed to have a supernatural power to exorcise evil spirits. *Nuo* drama masks are finely carved and richly shaped, generally divided into several types, namely, sacred deities, demons, worldly figures, and animals; and the colors are divided into two categories – light and powerful colors, which look very vibrant and decorous, yet simple and unsophisticatedly tasteful, giving rise to a rich national folk style.

Nuo drama masks depicting pestilence-dispelling deities

Di drama masks, Guizhou Province

Di Drama Mask

"*Di* drama" does not need a theatrical stage, but is performed in a village or open fields, hence its name (*di* means ground in Chinese). This theater genre is found mainly in areas over a radius of more than 100 kilometers around Anshun and Guiyang cities in Guizhou Province. *Di* drama has a long history of 600 to 700 years, the dramas performed mainly being based on historical stories. *Di* drama masks are made with high-quality white poplar, clove, gingko or *Catgalpa bungei* wood. The masks are finely carved, then color-painted with particular care, the most distinguished being the military officers.

Di drama masks (monk), Guizhou

Bi Xie

Bi xie is believed to be a mythical animal able to dispel demons, evil and wickedness. It has many images because of differences in materials and in places on which it is placed. It appears in the forms of ladles, masks and toys, as well as other architectural ornamentations. As architectural adornment, it was often placed on roofs or inside courtyards or the house, for the purpose of exorcizing evil and avoiding disasters.

Bi xie, collection of Gao Jinlong, Yunnan Province

Bi xie, collection of Gao Jinlong,
Yunnan Province

Bi xie, Guizhou

Ladle

The ladle is used to hold porridge or rice, and is usually made of wood.

Ladle, made by Li Jiyou, Shaanxi Province

DAILY-USE ARTICLES

Daily-use Articles

Cake mold symbolizing consecutive years of surplus

Lion-design cake mold

A patterned cake
mold depicting
"Unicorn Sending
A Son"

Cake mold with a pattern of peach,
inside which is
a character meaning longevity

A child-design cake mold

Cake mold with
auspicious-creature design

Tiered box,
Qingyunshan folk custom hall in
Weifang, Shandong Province

Red-lacquered tiered box
with the design of "Phoenix Flying
through Peony Flowers", Beijing

Red-lacquered tiered box
with the design of "Phoenix Flying through
Peony Flowers", Beijing

RELIGIOUS
WOODCARVINGS

Religious Woodcarvings

Statues of Deities

Images or statues of a deity or Buddha.

Dhanada
(or Vaisramana, god of rain)

Dhrtarastra
(god of gentle breeze)

Virupaka (god of good weather)

Virudhaka (god of wind)

Four Deva-kings (for favorable weather), gold-lacquer woodcarving, Meizhou, Fujian Province

Ma Zu (Lady Matriarch)

Ma Zu is the Goddess Tian Fei (Heavenly Imperial Concubine) or Tian Hou (Heavenly Empress). Ma Zu was said to have been born into the Lin family in Putian, Fujian Province, and because she did not cry one month after birth, her father gave her the name "Mo" (silence), and thus local people called her "Lady Lin Mo." She was said to be "a virtuous woman who could communicate with the gods." When young she had the blessings of Goddess of Mercy, and used to protect the townspeople when they went to sea, and ensured their safe return. She died in Putian at the age of 28, and since then has been worshipped as a "sea goddess." Ma Zu Temples are found everywhere in the three provinces of Fujian, Taiwan and Guangdong.

Ma Zu, created by Lin Yuansuo, Xianyou County, Fujian Province

Ma Zu, Xianyou County, Fujian Province

Ma Zu, Meizhou, Fujian Province

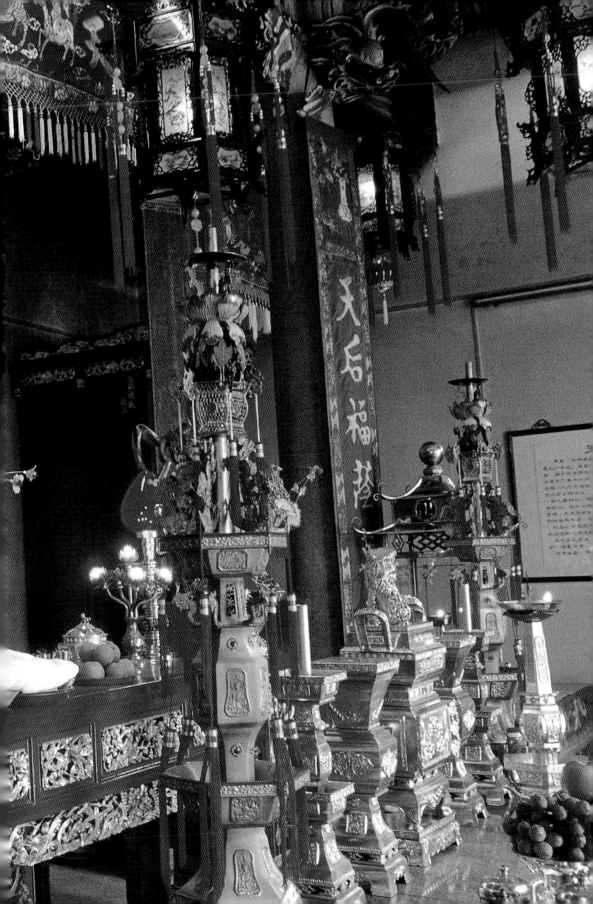

Guan Yu

Guan Yu (?-219), or Guan Yunchang, commonly known as Lord Guan, was a famous general of the State of Shu in the period of the Three Kingdom. He was highly venerated by the people due to his loyalty and righteousness, and came to be worshipped as a deity. Emperors throughout the ages constantly granted him titles, including giving him the additional titles of "Lord Guan" and "God of War." Guan Yu temples are found everywhere throughout the country. It is said that he is capable of protecting those who become wealthy, therefore he has been worshipped as the "God of Wealth."

Guan Yu, Yongding County, Fujian Province

Dragon King, Chengdu

Dragon Kings

Ancient people divided dragons into four categories: the heavenly dragon defending the heavens, the magic dragon that can generate cloud and rain, the earth dragon administering the different water sources on earth, and the treasure-trove dragon guarding treasures under heaven. The dragon kings worshiped by the folk refer mainly to the magic dragon and the earth dragon, which oversee floods and droughts as well as bumper and poor harvests in the human world. As soon as people were stricken by flood or drought disasters, they would go to the dragon-king temple to pray to the deities for blessings.

Goddess of Mercy

The Goddess of Mercy, also known as Avalokitesvara, is one of the Buddhist Bodhisattvas. It is said that the Goddess of Mercy has the power to transform herself into many images, such as a thousand-hands or thousand-eyes Bodhisattva. From the view of Buddhism, she can lift all living creatures out of hardship; as long as sufferers single-mindedly chant Buddhist sutras, the Goddess of Mercy would trace the voices and grant them help. The Goddess was originally endowed with a male body, but through circulating and evolving in the human world, later the Bodhisattva appeared mostly in a female image, with a boy well versed in handling financial affairs often standing by her side. The image of the Goddess is widely used in folk stone carving, porcelain sculpture, weaving and embroidery, as well as religious painting.

Goddess of Mercy, Xianyou, Fujian Province

Statue of Goddess of Mercy, Xianyou County, Fujian Province

God of Wealth

The God of Wealth Zhao Gongming was said to have been a man living in the Qin Dynasty (221-207). He obtained "*gati*" (direction of incarnation) on Shaanxi's Zhongnan Mountain. The Jade Emperor summoned and appointed him as "Deputy Marshal of Shen Xiao" (Heavenly Clouds), while Taoism has venerated him as "Marshal Zhao," hence people call him "the revered Marshal Zhao." Marshal Zhao was said to be able to eliminate pestilence and disaster, and administer people's finances, so people have worshipped him as a god of wealth. Zhao Gongming exercised command over the bringer of treasure Xiao Sheng (treasure collecting), Cao Bao (treasure keeping), Chen Jiugong (treasure delivering), and Yao Shaosi (profit-making). These five celestial beings are together called the "Five Gods of Wealth."

Marshal Zhao,
Anyang, Henan Province

Marshal Zhao, Chengdu

Shrine of the Kitchen God,
collection of Sun Jianjun

Kitchen God

The Kitchen God is said to be sent by the God of Heaven
to the human world to supervise people's daily conduct. In
Chinese tradition, there is the custom of worshipping the
Kitchen God on the 23rd of the 12th lunar month. On that
day, every household would have to put up a picture of the
Kitchen God, make sweet pastries, as well as burn incense
and make offerings, praying to the Kitchen God "to put in
a good word to the Jade Emperor for the people and return to his palace to bestow auspices upon them."

Fengma and Longda Flags

In the opinion of Tibetans, the profound meaning of *fengma* (wind horse) refers to a person's fortune and destiny. Places like holy mountains and sacred lakes are decorated with *fengma* flags printed with words expressing reverence for divinity and other prayers for blessings. The *longda* flags fluttering in the wind are believed to facilitate the transmission and realization of such wishes.

In Tibet and other regions where Tibetans live in compact communities, people can see everywhere strings of colored pennants, made with cloth, flax, silk and paper, with block-printed magic characters and incarnations. These square or triangular pennants are methodically fixed on doors and ropes by clan houses and on tree branches, fluttering and waving between the firmament and earth, symbolizing the linking of earth with heaven. Such pennants are called "*longda*" in Tibetan language, also referred to as "*ji ma*" (offerings to a horse), "*lu ma*" (lucky horse), "*jing fan*" (long narrow sutra flag) and "*qi yuan fan*" (prayers and wishes flag). However, people used to call them "*longda* flags," as in Tibetan language, "*long*" means "wind," and "*da*," "horse." "Wind horse" has its origins in ancient animist worship culture, coming mainly from the worshipping of animal spirits.

A Tibetan wood-carved plate

Wood-carved plate for printing
longda flags, Tibet

Wood-carved plate for printing
Fengma flags, Tibet

图书在版编目（CIP）数据

民间木雕：英文 / 王抗生编著；梁发明译 .
—北京：外文出版社，2009
（中国民间文化遗产）
ISBN 978-7-119-04679-2
I . 民... II . ①王... ②梁... III . 木雕—民间工艺—中国
—英文 IV.J314.2

中国版本图书馆 CIP 数据核字（2009）第 006885 号

出版策划：李振国
英文翻译：梁发明
英文审定：May Yee 王明杰
责任编辑：杨春燕
文案编辑：贾先锋 刘芳念
装帧设计：黎 红
印刷监制：韩少乙

本书由中国轻工业出版社授权出版

民间木雕

王抗生 编著

© 2009 外文出版社
出版发行：
外文出版社出版（中国北京百万庄大街 24 号）
邮政编码：100037
网 址：www.flp.com.cn
电 话：008610-68320579（总编室）
008610-68995852（发行部）
008610-68327750（版权部）
制 版：
北京维诺传媒文化有限公司

印 刷：
北京外文印刷厂

开 本：787mm×1092mm 1/16 印张：9.5
2009 年第 1 版第 1 次印刷
（英）
ISBN 978-7-119-04679-2
09800（平）
85-E-651 P